Boulder County Appraisement Book A 1875–1888

An Annotated Index

Compiled by Dina C. Carson

Boulder County Appraisement Book A
1875–1888

An Annotated Index

Compiled by Dina C. Carson

Published by:

Iron Gate Publishing
P.O. Box 999
Niwot, CO 80544

All rights reserved. No part of this book may be reproduced or transmitted in any form or by any means, electronic or mechanical, including photocopying, recording or any information storage and retrieval system without written permission from the author, except for the inclusion of brief quotations in a review.

The Publisher of this directory makes no representation that it is absolutely accurate or complete. Errors and omissions, whether typographical, clerical or otherwise do sometimes occur and may occur anywhere within the body of this publication. The Publisher does not assume and hereby disclaims any liability to any party for loss or damage by errors or omissions in this publication, whether such errors or omissions result from negligence, accident or any other cause.

Iron Gate Publishing has used its best efforts in collecting and preparing material for inclusion in the *Boulder County Appraisement Book A 1875-1888: An Annotated Index*, but does not warrant that the information herein is complete or accurate, and does not assume, and hereby disclaims, any liability to any person for any loss or damage caused by errors or ommissions in the *Boulder County Appraisement Book A 1875-1888: An Annotated Index*, whether such errors or omissions result from negligence, accident or any other cause.

Copyright © 2012 by Dina C. Carson, Iron Gate Publishing

Printed in the United States of America

	ISBN	1-879579-72-3	ISBN 13	978-1-879579-72-9
eBook	ISBN	1-879579-71-5	ISBN 13	978-1-879579-71-2

Introduction

In the Boulder County Probate Court's Appraisement Record, you will find the name of the deceased, the Judge and Sheriff charged with administering the appraisement of personal property, the administrator or executor of the estate, and the names of the appraisers of the estate (usually three).

Occasionally, you will find the name of a Justice of the Peace before whom the Appraisers took their oath, if different from the Judge charged with administering the appraisement or the Clerk of the County Court.

The Appraisers estimate also includes the value of property allowed to the widow including:

Beds, bedsteads and bedding for the widow and family
Wearing apparel of the widow and family
Household furniture for widow and family
Family pictures, school books and library
Stoves and appendages kept for use of the family
Cooking utensils
Household furntiture not enumerated, fixed value of $100
Provisions necessary for six months
Fuel necessary for six months
Working animals, fixed value of $200
1 cow and calf
10 sheep
1 horse, saddle and bridle
Necessary food for animals for six months
1 farm wagon, 1 plow, 1 harrow
Other farm implements, fixed value of $50

In later listings, allowances were also made for a seat or pew reserved within a house of worship, and the property on which to bury the dead.

The second page(s) of the Appraisement includes all articles appraised and their value, including livestock, land, household goods, farm implements, and ownership in businesses or mines.

Occasionally, you will find other people named if there are accounts owed or notes outstanding.

The Boulder County Assessor's Tax Record is held by the Colorado State Archives and is accessible for research. You can order a copy of pages from this Appraisement Book by calling the Colorado State Archives or placing an order through their website.

Boulder County Appraisement Book A, 1875–1888

1st National Bank of Boulder
pg 64 (1885 May 4)

1st National Bank of Gunnison
pg 64 (1885 May 4)

Aikins [Akins], Thos A
pg 21 (1878 July 15) deceased

Aikins [Akins], Thurston W
pg 21 (1878 July 15) Administrator

Albertson, Edward M
pg 58 (1884 Oct 14) Administrator

Albertson, Isabella
pg 58 (1884 Oct 14) deceased

Alice Lode
pg 79 (1886 July 6)

Allen, Almena A
pg 11 (1876 May 31) deceased

Allen, Gay S
pg 11 (1876 May 31) Executor

Allen, Jennie R
pg 95 (1887 Apr 18) Administratrix

Allen, Rudolphus N
pg 95 (1887 Apr 18) deceased

Anderson, Abraham
pg 31 (1880 Jan 21) deceased - no widow

Andrews, L E
pg 81 (1886 June 28) Administrator;
pg 82 (1886 Sept 9) Administrator

Arbuthnot, Samuel
pg 41 (1882 May 15) Administrator

Arbuthnot, William
pg 41 (1882 May 15) deceased

Armstrong, Frank
pg 56 (1884 Sept 15) deceased

Ash, P T
pg 95 (1887 Apr 18) account

Atkinson, John
pg 11 (1876 May 31) Appraiser

Atwood Farm
pg 75 (1886 Apr 5)

Autrey, Edward
pg 82 (1886 Sept 9) Appraiser

Autrey, Elijah
pg 23 (1878 Dec 10) Appraiser

Babcock, Eliza
pg 23 (1878 Dec 10) Administratrix

Babcock, Joseph
pg 23 (1878 Dec 10) deceased

Bader, J G
pg 41 (1882 May 15) Appraiser

Bagley, M A
pg 72 (1886 Mar 3) Appraiser

Baldwin, Charles
pg 39 (1881 Dec 31) account

Baldwin, Charles G
pg 70 (1885 Dec 15) deceased

Baldwin, Frances A
pg 70 (1885 Dec 15) Administratrix

Baldwin, L E
pg 30 (1879 Dec 31) Appraiser

Boulder County Appraisement Book A, 1875–1888

Bank of Central
pg 4 (1875 Dec 20) note owed

Banks, F B
pg 43 (1883 Jan 2) Justice of the Peace; pg 43 (1883 Jan 2) Administrator

Barclay, S J
pg 39 (1881 Dec 31) account

Barker, Ezra
pg 18 (1878 Apr 11) deceased - no widow

Barker, Ezra K
pg 18 (1878 Apr 11) Administrator; pg 44 (1883 Feb 23) deceased

Barker, Hannah C
pg 44 (1883 Feb 23) Administratrix

Barnes, Thomas H
pg 36 (1880 Nov 5) Appraiser

Barron No. 2 Lode
pg 79 (1886 July 6)

Barthoff & Bushnell
pg 39 (1881 Dec 31) account

Bartlett, John H
pg 102 (1887 Sept 16) deceased

Bashor, Franklin
pg 97 (1887 May 4) deceased

Bashor, M E
pg 95 (1887 Apr 18) account

Bashor, Madison
pg 97 (1887 May 4) Appraiser

Basten, Thomas
pg 34 (1880 Apr 1) Justice of the Peace

Batchelder, George H
pg 16 (1878 Feb 18) Appraiser

Bates Co. Natl Bank of Missouri
pg 64 (1885 May 4)

Baxter
pg 39 (1881 Dec 31) account

Beardsley, Alexander B
pg 14 (1877 Aug 23) deceased

Beardsley, Lovina
pg 14 (1877 Aug 23) Administratrix

Beasley & Fitch
pg 95 (1887 Apr 18) account

Beasley, J J
pg 72 (1886 Mar 3) Appraiser

Belcher, Freeman
pg 70 (1885 Dec 15) Appraiser

Bellman, John
pg 39 (1881 Dec 31) account

Bergstrom, J
pg 31 (1880 Jan 21) account

Berkley, G
pg 12 (1877 Feb 20) Appraiser

Berkley, Granville Sr
pg 55 (1884 Aug 20) deceased ; pg 62 (1885 Apr 1) deceased

Berkley, Junius
pg 55 (1884 Aug 20) Administrator

Boulder County Appraisement Book A, 1875–1888

Berlin, Isaac
pg 90 (1887 Feb 14) Administrator

Bever Ditch
pg 8 (1876 June 20) 3 shares

Bigger, R A
pg 78 (1886 July 6) Appraiser; pg 79 (1886 July 6) Appraiser

Billings, Geo
pg 39 (1881 Dec 31) account

Bird, J H
pg 4 (1875 Dec 20) note owed - secured by first deed

Bixby, Amos
pg 44 (1883 Feb 23) Appraiser

Bixby, J H
pg 64 (1885 May 4) note

Blake, Frank O
pg 38 (1881 June 23) Appraiser; pg 73 (1886 Mar 26) Appraiser; pg 92 (1887 Mar 23) Notary Public; pg 105 (1887 May 23) Notary Public

Blake, Henry
pg 38 (1881 June 23) Appraiser

Bond, Isaac L
pg 57 (1884 Sept 12) Administrator; pg 72 (1886 Mar 3) Administrator; pg 86 (1886 Nov 29) Administrator

Borden, Edmund J
pg 58 (1884 Oct 14) Notary Public; pg 76 (1886 June 2) Appraiser; pg 84 (1886 Oct 2) Justice of the Peace

Boulder Co. Indust Assn
pg 64 (1885 May 4)

Boulder, Left Hand and M P R R Co
pg 64 (1885 May 4)

Boylen, R
pg 28 (1879 Aug 15) Appraiser

Brace, C C
pg 92 (1887 Mar 23) Appraiser

Bradford, Chas
pg 77 (1886 May 20) Appraiser

Bramwood, William
pg 57 (1884 Sept 12) deceased; pg 72 (1886 Mar 3) deceased - no widow; pg 86 (1886 Nov 29) deceased

Breath, S M
pg 44 (1883 Feb 23) Appraiser

Brown, George W
pg 60 (1884 Nov 24) Appraiser

Bruce, Ellen
pg 52 (1884 May 15) deceased; pg 73 (1886 Mar 26) deceased

Bruce, George D
pg 52 (1884 May 15) Administrator; pg 73 (1886 Mar 26) Administrator

Buckingham, Mary E
pg 39 (1881 Dec 31) Administratrix

Buckingham, Walter A
pg 39 (1881 Dec 31) deceased

Boulder County Appraisement Book A, 1875–1888

Budd, Sylvanus
pg 42 (1882 Aug 23) Appraiser; pg 48 (1884 Jan 28) Appraiser; pg 80 (1886 July 28) Appraiser

Burch, Leonard
pg 75 (1886 Apr 5) Appraiser

Burger
pg 95 (1887 Apr 18) account

Burke, William
pg 4 (1875 Dec 20) note owed - no security for this note

Burnham, Ida W
pg 63 (1885 May 9) Administratrix

Burnham, Levi
pg 63 (1885 May 9) deceased

Burns, Edward
pg 16 (1878 Feb 18) Administrator

Burns, William H
pg 16 (1878 Feb 18) deceased - no widow

Butter, Thomas
pg 8 (1876 June 20) Justice of the Peace

Calcutt, J V
pg 9 (1875 Dec 3) Administrator

Calkins, C C
pg 95 (1887 Apr 18) account

Callahan, D D
pg 46 (1883 Dec 17) Appraiser

Campbell, Alexander
pg 59 (1884 Nov 8) Appraiser

Campbell, Charles M
pg 11 (1876 May 31) Appraiser; pg 14 (1877 Aug 23) Appraiser; pg 76 (1886 June 2) Appraiser

Campbell, D C
pg 18 (1878 Apr 11) Appraiser

Cannon, J A
pg 39 (1881 Dec 31) account

Carr, Byron L
pg 5 (1875 Nov 12) Administrator; pg 5 (1875 Nov 12) Notary Public

Carr, Eugene H
pg 9 (1875 Dec 3) Notary Public

Carrier, Elizabeth S
pg 60 (1884 Nov 24) deceased

Case, Carrie E
pg 69 (1885 Dec 31) Administratrix

Case, W H H
pg 69 (1885 Dec 31) deceased

Cave, James
pg 64 (1885 May 4) note

Caywood, Ada
pg 35 (1880 Apr 1) Administratrix

Caywood, Richard F
pg 35 (1880 Apr 1) deceased

Caywood, Sam
pg 95 (1887 Apr 18) account

Chambers, George W
pg 21 (1878 July 15) Appraiser; pg 36 (1880 Nov 5) Justice of the Peace; pg 71 (1886 Mar 16) Appraiser

Boulder County Appraisement Book A, 1875–1888

Chambers, John S
pg 47 (1883 Oct 25) Administrator; pg 82 (1886 Sept 9) Appraiser

Chapman, Joshua E
pg 8 (1876 June 20) Administrator

Chapman, Volney
pg 10 (1876 Mar 13) Appraiser; pg 28 (1879 Aug 15) Appraiser

Chase & Sears
pg 3 (1875 Nov 5) Central City business

Chase, George F
pg 17 (1878 Apr 30) Appraiser; pg 44 (1883 Feb 23) Appraiser; pg 103 (1887 Nov 13) Appraiser

Chase, Lyman W
pg 32 (1880 Feb 3) deceased - no widow

Chedsey, Herbert
pg 17 (1878 Apr 30) Appraiser

Cheney & Milner
pg 64 (1885 May 4)

Cheney, Lewis
pg 64 (1885 May 4) deceased

Cheney, R
pg 64 (1885 May 4) note

Chittenden, Albert C
pg 17 (1878 Apr 30) deceased

Chittenden, Patience L
pg 17 (1878 Apr 30) Administratrix

Church, George H
pg 88 (1887 Jan 25) Administrator

Church, John L
pg 55 (1884 Aug 20) Appraiser; pg 62 (1885 Apr 1) Appraiser; pg 88 (1887 Jan 25) Administrator

Clark, C A
pg 40 (1882 Feb 27) Justice of the Peace; pg 47 (1883 Oct 25) Justice of the Peace; pg 81 (1886 June 28) Appraiser

Clarke, W A
pg 15 (1877 Oct 2) Appraiser

Clawson, Wm
pg 95 (1887 Apr 18) account

Clemens, Susan
pg 54 (1883 Dec 17) Administratrix

Clemens, Theodore
pg 54 (1883 Dec 17) deceased

Coan, Alonzo
pg 19 (1878 Apr 15) Administrator

Coffman, Arthur W
pg 7 (1876 June 6) Executor

Coffman, Jacob T
pg 7 (1876 June 6) deceased

Coffman, Mary P
pg 7 (1876 June 6) Executor

Compton, T B
pg 76 (1886 June 2) Appraiser

Connecting Link Lode
pg 79 (1886 July 6)

Cooper, C E
pg 95 (1887 Apr 18) account

Corbett, Ed
pg 95 (1887 Apr 18) account

Corrie, James
pg 93 (1887 Apr 14) Appraiser

Corson, William A
pg 6 (1876 May 8) Appraiser

Coulehan, James C
pg 96 (1887 Apr 25) deceased

Coulehan, Miranda
pg 96 (1887 Apr 25) Administratrix

Courmerford, M J
pg 65 (1885 May 26) Appraiser

Cowdery, George W
pg 47 (1883 Oct 25) deceased - no widow

Cowdery, Henry A
pg 47 (1883 Oct 25) Administrator

Crane, H C
pg 16 (1878 Feb 18) Justice of the Peace

Cranson, John
pg 89 (1887 Jan 15) deceased

Crossley, John
pg 9 (1875 Dec 3) deceased

Culinglet, L C
pg 95 (1887 Apr 18) account

Cullacott, John J
pg 78 (1886 July 6) insane - Saloon owner; pg 79 (1886 July 6) insane

Cummerford, M J
pg 100 (1887 Sept 7) Appraiser

Cummings, T
pg 95 (1887 Apr 18) account

Cushman, A G (Mrs)
pg 95 (1887 Apr 18) account

Cushman, A W
pg 97 (1887 May 4) Appraiser

Custner, Wm
pg 100 (1887 Sept 7) Appraiser

Daily, Andy
pg 95 (1887 Apr 18) account

Davidson Ditch Co.
pg 87 (1887 Jan 20)

Davis, Chas D
pg 26 (1878 Dec 14) Notary Public

Davis, David
pg 2 (1875 Apr 14) Appraiser

Davis, George F
pg 57 (1884 Sept 12) Appraiser; pg 86 (1886 Nov 29) Appraiser

Dawley, James M
pg 2 (1875 Apr 14) Notary Public; pg 2 (1875 Apr 14) Administrator

Day, Charles E
pg 39 (1881 Dec 31) Appraiser; pg 95 (1887 Apr 18) Appraiser

Day, John W
pg 73 (1886 Mar 26) Appraiser; pg 76 (1886 June 2) Notary Public; pg 76 (1886 June 2) Executor

Boulder County Appraisement Book A, 1875–1888

DeBacker, John
pg 46 (1883 Dec 17) Appraiser

Decker, J H
pg 1 (1875 Apr 12) Judge; pg 2 (1875 Apr 14) Judge

Deering, D Y H
pg 20 (1878 May 31) Appraiser

Deitz, Henry
pg 33 (1880 Feb 21) Appraiser

Dell, George T
pg 74 (1886 Apr 23) Appraiser; pg 89 (1887 Jan 15) Executor

Dickens, W H
pg 70 (1885 Dec 15) Appraiser

Dickson, Lewis H
pg 61 (1884 Dec 18) Appraiser; pg 88 (1887 Jan 25) Appraiser

Dixon, Charles
pg 40 (1882 Feb 27) Appraiser

Dolloff, Levi W
pg 35 (1880 Apr 1) Justice of the Peace

Donald, William
pg 3 (1875 Nov 5) Appraiser; pg 93 (1887 Apr 14) Administrator

Donelley, Leo
pg 3 (1875 Nov 5) Appraiser; pg 4 (1875 Dec 20) note owed - secured by property at Caribou

Dorsey, Mathew
pg 47 (1883 Oct 25) Appraiser

Dowie, James
pg 53 (1884 May 19) Appraiser

Downer, Francis M
pg 39 (1881 Dec 31) Appraiser; pg 95 (1887 Apr 18) Notary Public

Downer, Sylvester S
pg 37 (1881 June 6) Judge; pg 38 (1881 June 23) Judge; pg 39 (1881 Dec 31) Judge; pg 40 (1882 Feb 27) Judge; pg 41 (1882 May 15) Judge ; pg 42 (1882 Aug 23) Judge; pg 43 (1883 Jan 2) Judge; pg 44 (1883 Feb 23) Judge; pg 45 (1883 Apr 30) Judge; pg 46 (1883 Dec 17) Judge; pg 47 (1883 Oct 25) Judge; pg 48 (1884 Jan 28) Judge; pg 49 (1884 Feb 5) Judge; pg 50 (1884 Feb 11) Judge; pg 51 (1884 May 10) Judge; pg 52 (1884 May 15) Judge; pg 53 (1884 May 19) Judge; pg 54 (1883 Dec 17) Judge; pg 55 (1884 Aug 20) Judge; pg 56 (1884 Sept 15) Judge; pg 57 (1884 Sept 12) Judge; pg 58 (1884 Oct 14) Judge; pg 59 (1884 Nov 8) Judge; pg 60 (1884 Nov 24) Judge; pg 61 (1884 Dec 18) Judge; pg 62 (1885 Apr 1) Judge; pg 63 (1885 May 9) Judge; pg 64 (1885 May 4) Judge; pg 65 (1885 May 26) Judge; pg 66 (1885 July 29) Judge; pg 67 (1885 Aug 21) Judge; pg 68 (1885 Sept 8) Judge

Dunagan, Elijah
pg 53 (1884 May 19) deceased

Dunn, Margaret
pg 87 (1887 Jan 20) deceased

Dunn, Philip D
pg 87 (1887 Jan 20) Administrator

Durfram Idaho Co
pg 4 (1875 Dec 20) note owed - for wood, shingles

Dusty Diamond Lode
pg 79 (1886 July 6)

Dwyer, Harry
pg 83 (1886 Sept 13) Appraiser

Dycer, William
pg 99 (1887 July 22) deceased

Earhart, W R
pg 63 (1885 May 9) Appraiser

Eggleston, George W
pg 23 (1878 Dec 10) Appraiser

Eisele, John J
pg 101 (1887 Sept 12) deceased - no widow

Eldred, F H
pg 105 (1887 May 23) Appraiser

Ellet, John A
pg 71 (1886 Mar 16) Notary Public; pg 73 (1886 Mar 26) Appraiser

Ellingham, John J
pg 17 (1878 Apr 30) Sheriff; pg 18 (1878 Apr 11) Sheriff; pg 19 (1878 Apr 15) Sheriff; pg 20 (1878 May 31) Sheriff; pg 21 (1878 July 15) Sheriff; pg 30 (1879 Dec 31) Sheriff; pg 31 (1880 Jan 21) Sheriff; pg 32 (1880 Feb 3) Sheriff; pg 33 (1880 Feb 21) Sheriff; pg 34 (1880 Apr 1) Sheriff; pg 35 (1880 Apr 1) Sheriff; pg 37 (1881 June 6) Sheriff

Emerson & Buckingham
pg 39 (1881 Dec 31)

Errickson, Andrew P
pg 12 (1877 Feb 20) deceased

Errickson, Eva
pg 12 (1877 Feb 20) Administratrix

Evans, G I
pg 39 (1881 Dec 31) account

Evans, Grif
pg 95 (1887 Apr 18) account

Fairhurst, Guy
pg 100 (1887 Sept 7) Appraiser

Fanning Mill
pg 88 (1887 Jan 25)

Farley, Jas
pg 39 (1881 Dec 31) account

Farmer's Ditch Co.
pg 12 (1877 Feb 20); pg 62 (1885 Apr 1)

Fee, E S
pg 29 (1879 Sept 3) Appraiser

Ferham, Ann
pg 4 (1875 Dec 20) note owed - Ferham son, note secured by property at Black Hawk

Fink, George
pg 27 (1879 Jan 15) Appraiser

Boulder County Appraisement Book A, 1875–1888

Finley, Joseph J
pg 63 (1885 May 9) Notary Public

First National Bank
pg 4 (1875 Dec 20) note owed

Flansburg, Isaac
pg 89 (1887 Jan 15) Appraiser

Fonda, Geo F
pg 96 (1887 Apr 25) Appraiser

Foote, James B
pg 27 (1879 Jan 15) Appraiser; pg 32 (1880 Feb 3) Appraiser; pg 105 (1887 May 23) Appraiser

Fowler, W B
pg 30 (1879 Dec 31) Appraiser

Fox, Michael P
pg 50 (1884 Feb 11) Justice of the Peace; pg 104 (1887 Nov 12) Administrator

Frank, Nicholas
pg 83 (1886 Sept 13) Executor

Franklin, R Q
pg 95 (1887 Apr 18) note

Franklin, W J
pg 95 (1887 Apr 18) note

Franklin, William
pg 22 (1878 June 17) Appraiser; pg 95 (1887 Apr 18) account

Fuller, J G
pg 33 (1880 Feb 21) Appraiser

Galusha, S S
pg 4 (1875 Dec 20) note owed

Garrison, J T
pg 49 (1884 Feb 5) Justice of the Peace

Gibson, H P
pg 61 (1884 Dec 18) Appraiser

Giffin, S A
pg 55 (1884 Aug 20) Appraiser; pg 62 (1885 Apr 1) Appraiser; pg 64 (1885 May 4) Appraiser

Giles, George W
pg 47 (1883 Oct 25) Appraiser

Gilman, Stephen
pg 34 (1880 Apr 1) Appraiser

Gordon, James
pg 19 (1878 Apr 15) deceased - non-resident

Gould, James B
pg 13 (1877 July 7) Appraiser; pg 21 (1878 July 15) Appraiser

Gould, Jerome
pg 48 (1884 Jan 28) Appraiser

Goyn, Richard
pg 41 (1882 May 15) Appraiser

Graham, Thomas J
pg 6 (1876 May 8) Administrator; pg 6 (1876 May 8) Notary Public

Grand Duke Lode
pg 16 (1878 Feb 18) Boulder Cty

Grand Union Mining Lode
pg 72 (1886 Mar 3) Central Mining District

Boulder County Appraisement Book A, 1875–1888

Green, R L & Bros
pg 95 (1887 Apr 18) account

Groesbeck, Abram
pg 28 (1879 Aug 15) deceased

Groesbeck, J B
pg 1 (1875 Apr 12) Executor

Groesbeck, Orinda R
pg 28 (1879 Aug 15) Administratrix

Guinwood, Charles L
pg 9 (1875 Dec 3) Appraiser

Guise, James H
pg 45 (1883 Apr 30) Appraiser

Guise, Jas H
pg 101 (1887 Sept 12) Appraiser

Gummerson, S
pg 31 (1880 Jan 21) account

Hague, John H
pg 97 (1887 May 4) Executor

Hall, Horace C
pg 58 (1884 Oct 14) Appraiser

Hall, Ira F
pg 5 (1875 Nov 12) Appraiser

Hall, T A
pg 66 (1885 July 29) Appraiser

Hanby, James M
pg 77 (1886 May 20) Appraiser

Handy Ditch Co
pg 39 (1881 Dec 31)

Hankins, J C
pg 52 (1884 May 15) Appraiser

Hansbrough, Oliver C Esq
pg 19 (1878 Apr 15) Appraiser; pg 104 (1887 Nov 12) Sheriff; pg 105 (1887 May 23) Sheriff

Harlow, L K
pg 17 (1878 Apr 30) Appraiser

Hartman, A
pg 64 (1885 May 4) note

Haskin, H A
pg 54 (1883 Dec 17) Appraiser

Hays, Nancy S
pg 13 (1877 July 7) deceased

Healey, Marthy A
pg 30 (1879 Dec 31) Administratrix

Healey, Nathan M
pg 30 (1879 Dec 31) deceased

Heller, Thos A
pg 103 (1887 Nov 13) Appraiser

Henry, A T
pg 32 (1880 Feb 3) Administrator

Hepburn, Henry
pg 4 (1875 Dec 20) note owed - supposed to be settled

Hepburn, Mary
pg 4 (1875 Dec 20) note owed - secured by trust deed

Herron, O F
pg 74 (1886 Apr 23) Appraiser

Hersey, J Clarence
pg 13 (1877 July 7) Administrator

13

Boulder County Appraisement Book A, 1875–1888

Hetzer, J W
pg 53 (1884 May 19) Appraiser

Hickey, John B
pg 52 (1884 May 15) Appraiser

Hickey, P J
pg 87 (1887 Jan 20) Appraiser

Hickock
pg 39 (1881 Dec 31) account

Hicks, C D
pg 4 (1875 Dec 20) note owed - no security for this note

Higbee, Fred L
pg 59 (1884 Nov 8) Appraiser

Highland Ditch Co
pg 39 (1881 Dec 31); pg 86 (1886 Nov 29)

Hinman, Estelle T
pg 48 (1884 Jan 28) Administratrix (see also, Smith, Estelle T Hinman)

Hinman, M L
pg 41 (1882 May 15) Appraiser

Hinman, Porter M
pg 48 (1884 Jan 28) deceased; pg 80 (1886 July 28) deceased

Hogan, John
pg 51 (1884 May 10) Appraiser; pg 50 (1884 Feb 11) Appraiser; pg 87 (1887 Jan 20) Appraiser

Holcomb, John B
pg 83 (1886 Sept 13) Appraiser

Holding, Robt
pg 45 (1883 Apr 30) Justice of the Peace

Holland, Will
pg 95 (1887 Apr 18) account

Hornbaker, Wm
pg 80 (1886 July 28) Appraiser

Horner, J W
pg 62 (1885 Apr 1) Trustee

Housel, P M
pg 13 (1877 July 7) Appraiser

Howard, N R
pg 104 (1887 Nov 12) Appraiser

Howe, Ira
pg 37 (1881 June 6) deceased - no widow

Hubbard, James
pg 10 (1876 Mar 13) deceased

Hughes, James
pg 53 (1884 May 19) Administrator

Hull, Ira
pg 22 (1878 June 17) deceased - no widow

Hunt, F A
pg 15 (1877 Oct 2) Appraiser

Hupper, Elias A
pg 2 (1875 Apr 14) Appraiser; pg 4 (1875 Dec 20) Appraiser

Irish World Lode
pg 79 (1886 July 6)

Irwin, Joseph
pg 43 (1883 Jan 2) Appraiser

Jackson, John
pg 13 (1877 July 7) Appraiser

Johnson, B M
pg 85 (1886 Oct 19) Appraiser

Johnson, Nelson
pg 31 (1880 Jan 21) note

Johnson, Peter J
pg 31 (1880 Jan 21) Appraiser; pg 67 (1885 Aug 21) Appraiser; pg 85 (1886 Oct 19) Appraiser

Johnson, Seymour
pg 43 (1883 Jan 2) Appraiser

Johnson, Thomas C
pg 45 (1883 Apr 30) Appraiser

Jones Lode
pg 16 (1878 Feb 18) Gilpin Cty

Jones, James F
pg 81 (1886 June 28) Appraiser

Joseph Lloyd
pg 93 (1887 Apr 14) Appraiser

Kansas Lode
pg 79 (1886 July 6)

Katzanmayer, John Ernest
pg 9 (1875 Dec 3) Appraiser

Keen, Ann D
pg 34 (1880 Apr 1) Administratrix

Keen, John F
pg 34 (1880 Apr 1) deceased

Kellogg, W W
pg 22 (1878 June 17) Notary Public

Kerr, David
pg 46 (1883 Dec 17) Appraiser

Kerr, Thomas
pg 56 (1884 Sept 15) Appraiser

King William Lode
pg 79 (1886 July 6)

King, James A
pg 21 (1878 July 15) Appraiser

Kirby, John
pg 102 (1887 Sept 16) Appraiser

Kirkbride, Geo
pg 101 (1887 Sept 12) Appraiser

Kitely, John
pg 5 (1875 Nov 12) Appraiser; pg 7 (1876 June 6) Appraiser

Koehler, Louis
pg 29 (1879 Sept 3) Appraiser

Kohler, Frederick W
pg 10 (1876 Mar 13) Appraiser; pg 50 (1884 Feb 11) Appraiser; pg 51 (1884 May 10) Appraiser; pg 84 (1886 Oct 2) Appraiser

Kotenio, Kelly
pg 4 (1875 Dec 20) note owed

LaCroix, Evaniste
pg 9 (1875 Dec 3) Appraiser

Lafferty, T J
pg 54 (1883 Dec 17) Appraiser

Boulder County Appraisement Book A, 1875–1888

Lafourcade, William R
pg 59 (1884 Nov 8) deceased

Larson, A P
pg 31 (1880 Jan 21) note; pg 67 (1885 Aug 21) Appraiser

Larson, Carl I
pg 67 (1885 Aug 21) deceased; pg 85 (1886 Oct 19) deceased

Larson, John P
pg 100 (1887 Sept 7) deceased - no widow

Lea, Alfred E
pg 37 (1881 June 6) Administrator; pg 45 (1883 Apr 30) Administrator

Leah May Lode
pg 79 (1886 July 6)

Lee, Leim
pg 95 (1887 Apr 18) account

Leedy, Daniel
pg 97 (1887 May 4) Appraiser

Left Hand Ditch Co.
pg 64 (1885 May 4)

Leggett, Jeremiah
pg 49 (1884 Feb 5) Appraiser

Leonard, John
pg 88 (1887 Jan 25) deceased

Likens, W W
pg 46 (1883 Dec 17) Notary Public

Loch, Robert
pg 82 (1886 Sept 9) Appraiser

Logan, Henry
pg 28 (1879 Aug 15) Notary Public

Luther, Sam
pg 95 (1887 Apr 18) account

Lykins, David J
pg 34 (1880 Apr 1) Appraiser

Lyman, R R
pg 10 (1876 Mar 13) Executor

Macky, A J
pg 64 (1885 May 4) Appraiser

Mann, J W
pg 39 (1881 Dec 31) account

Maroney, Ann
pg 4 (1875 Dec 20) note owed - secured by first deed

Marshall Ditch Co.
pg 87 (1887 Jan 20)

Martin, Dr
pg 95 (1887 Apr 18) account

Martin, M G
pg 95 (1887 Apr 18) account

Martin, William
pg 104 (1887 Nov 12) Appraiser

Mason, Chris A
pg 100 (1887 Sept 7) Administrator

Mathews, A A
pg 74 (1886 Apr 23) Appraiser

Matthews, James J
pg 37 (1881 June 6) Appraiser

Matthews, Johnny
pg 95 (1887 Apr 18) account

Matthews, M & M
pg 64 (1885 May 4) note

Mattison, Ed
pg 95 (1887 Apr 18) account

Maud, Walter
pg 95 (1887 Apr 18) account

Maxwell, James P
pg 4 (1875 Dec 20) note owed - second on property in Boulder City; pg 37 (1881 June 6) Appraiser; pg 38 (1881 June 23) Administrator; pg 75 (1886 Apr 5) Executor; pg 92 (1887 Mar 23) Executor

Maxwell, John M
pg 15 (1877 Oct 2) Notary Public

May, George W
pg 102 (1887 Sept 16) Appraiser

McAllister, J T
pg 52 (1884 May 15) Appraiser

McCall, Thomas
pg 68 (1885 Sept 8) deceased

McCall, William A
pg 12 (1877 Feb 20) Appraiser

McCaslin, M L
pg 42 (1882 Aug 23) Appraiser

McDearman, Joseph H
pg 58 (1884 Oct 14) Appraiser

McDowell, Edward B
pg 59 (1884 Nov 8) Administrator

McGann, Simon
pg 50 (1884 Feb 11) deceased; pg 51 (1884 May 10) deceased

McIntosh, Jas P
pg 90 (1887 Feb 14) Appraiser

McIntosh, Lemuel
pg 84 (1886 Oct 2) Appraiser; pg 88 (1887 Jan 25) Appraiser; pg 104 (1887 Nov 12) Appraiser

McKenzie, William
pg 23 (1878 Dec 10) Appraiser

McLane
pg 39 (1881 Dec 31) account

Mead, L C
pg 39 (1881 Dec 31) account

Meginnis, D
pg 32 (1880 Feb 3) Appraiser; pg 33 (1880 Feb 21) Appraiser

Merriman, John F
pg 5 (1875 Nov 12) deceased

Metcalf, Eli P Esq
pg 48 (1884 Jan 28) Sheriff; pg 49 (1884 Feb 5) Sheriff; pg 50 (1884 Feb 11) Sheriff; pg 51 (1884 May 10) Sheriff; pg 53 (1884 May 19) Sheriff; pg 54 (1883 Dec 17) Sheriff; pg 55 (1884 Aug 20) Sheriff; pg 57 (1884 Sept 12) Sheriff; pg 56 (1884 Sept 15) Sheriff; pg 58 (1884 Oct 14) Sheriff; pg 52 (1884 May 15) Sheriff; pg 59 (1884 Nov 8) Sheriff; pg 60 (1884 Nov 24) Sheriff; pg 61 (1884 Dec 18) Sheriff; pg 62 (1885 Apr 1) Sheriff; pg 63 (1885 May 9) Sheriff;

Boulder County Appraisement Book A, 1875–1888

pg 64 (1885 May 4) Sheriff; pg 65 (1885 May 26) Sheriff; pg 66 (1885 July 29) Sheriff; pg 67 (1885 Aug 21) Sheriff; pg 68 (1885 Sept 8) Sheriff; pg 69 (1885 Dec 31) Sheriff; pg 70 (1885 Dec 15) Sheriff; pg 71 (1886 Mar 16) Sheriff; pg 72 (1886 Mar 3) Sheriff; pg 73 (1886 Mar 26) Sheriff; pg 74 (1886 Apr 23) Sheriff; pg 75 (1886 Apr 5) Sheriff; pg 76 (1886 June 2) Sheriff; pg 77 (1886 May 20) Sheriff; pg 78 (1886 July 6) Sheriff; pg 79 (1886 July 6) Sheriff; pg 80 (1886 July 28) Sheriff; pg 81 (1886 June 28) Sheriff; pg 82 (1886 Sept 9) Sheriff; pg 83 (1886 Sept 13) Sheriff; pg 84 (1886 Oct 2) Sheriff; pg 85 (1886 Oct 19) Sheriff; pg 86 (1886 Nov 29) Sheriff; pg 87 (1887 Jan 20) Sheriff; pg 88 (1887 Jan 25) Sheriff; pg 89 (1887 Jan 15) Sheriff; pg 90 (1887 Feb 14) Sheriff; pg 91 (1887 Mar 15) Sheriff; pg 92 (1887 Mar 23) Sheriff; pg 93 (1887 Apr 14) Sheriff; pg 95 (1887 Apr 18) Sheriff; pg 96 (1887 Apr 25) Sheriff; pg 97 (1887 May 4) Sheriff; pg 98 (1887 May 23) Sheriff; pg 99 (1887 July 22) Sheriff; pg 100 (1887 Sept 7) Sheriff; pg 101 (1887 Sept 12) Sheriff; pg 102 (1887 Sept 16) Sheriff; pg 103 (1887 Nov 13) Sheriff

Metcalf, L
pg 39 (1881 Dec 31) account

Meyring, Henry
pg 78 (1886 July 6) Appraiser; pg 79 (1886 July 6) Appraiser

Miller, J C
pg 4 (1875 Dec 20) note owed - second on property at Caribou

Miller, John S
pg 42 (1882 Aug 23) deceased

Miller, Lafayette
pg 27 (1879 Jan 15) deceased

Miller, Mary E
pg 27 (1879 Jan 15) Administratrix

Miller, Sarah E
pg 42 (1882 Aug 23) Administratix

Miners Vault Lode
pg 79 (1886 July 6)

Mischler, Samuel
pg 4 (1875 Dec 20) Administrator

Mitchell, Wm E
pg 78 (1886 July 6) Appraiser; pg 79 (1886 July 6) Appraiser

Moffitt, B D
pg 59 (1884 Nov 8) Appraiser

Montgomery, Robert
pg 18 (1878 Apr 11) Appraiser

Moore, J S
pg 19 (1878 Apr 15) Appraiser

Moore, Mary C
pg 71 (1886 Mar 16) Administratrix

Moore, Robert A
pg 71 (1886 Mar 16) deceased

Moore, Wm
pg 69 (1885 Dec 31) Appraiser

Boulder County Appraisement Book A, 1875–1888

Morath, Edward J
pg 12 (1877 Feb 20) Clerk; pg 13 (1877 July 7) Clerk; pg 14 (1877 Aug 23) Clerk; pg 38 (1881 June 23) Appraiser

Morger, Mary E
pg 74 (1886 Apr 23) Administratrix

Morger, Romantis B
pg 74 (1886 Apr 23) deceased - saloon owner

Mork, John J
pg 31 (1880 Jan 21) Administrator; pg 67 (1885 Aug 21) Administrator; pg 85 (1886 Oct 19) Administrator

Mork, Ole J
pg 42 (1882 Aug 23) Appraiser

Morrow, Susan A
pg 76 (1886 June 2) deceased

Morton, James
pg 40 (1882 Feb 27) Administrator

Morton, John
pg 40 (1882 Feb 27) deceased - no widow

Murphy, Joseph J
pg 93 (1887 Apr 14) Appraiser

Mutual Life Insurance Company of New York
pg 36 (1880 Nov 5)

Neeley, Wm B
pg 35 (1880 Apr 1) Appraiser

Nelson, A J
pg 31 (1880 Jan 21) note

Nelson, J H
pg 31 (1880 Jan 21) note; pg 31 (1880 Jan 21) account

Newland, Mary E
pg 84 (1886 Oct 2) Administratrix

Newland, William
pg 84 (1886 Oct 2) deceased

Nicholson, J H
pg 91 (1887 Mar 15) Appraiser

Nielsson, Johannes
pg 67 (1885 Aug 21) Appraiser; pg 85 (1886 Oct 19) Appraiser

Noland, Thomas H
pg 54 (1883 Dec 17) Justice of the Peace

North, James M
pg 16 (1878 Feb 18) Judge; pg 17 (1878 Apr 30) Judge; pg 18 (1878 Apr 11) Judge; pg 19 (1878 Apr 15) Judge; pg 20 (1878 May 31) Judge; pg 21 (1878 July 15) Judge; pg 22 (1878 June 17) Judge; pg 23 (1878 Dec 10) Judge; pg 26 (1878 Dec 14) Judge; pg 27 (1879 Jan 15) Judge; pg 28 (1879 Aug 15) Judge; pg 29 (1879 Sept 3) Judge; pg 30 (1879 Dec 31) Judge; pg 31 (1880 Jan 21) Judge; pg 32 (1880 Feb 3) Judge; pg 33 (1880 Feb 21) Judge; pg 34 (1880 Apr 1) Judge; pg 35 (1880 Apr 1) Judge; pg 36 (1880 Nov 5) Judge

Olander, A
pg 31 (1880 Jan 21) account

Boulder County Appraisement Book A, 1875–1888

Olander, August
pg 31 (1880 Jan 21) Appraiser

Oliver, Geo S
pg 91 (1887 Mar 15) Notary Public

Oliver, W H
pg 99 (1887 July 22) Appraiser

Orahood, Harper M
pg 4 (1875 Dec 20) Appraiser - Gilpin Cty

Orvis, Harrison F
pg 1 (1875 Apr 12) Appraiser

Otis, Emma A P
pg 36 (1880 Nov 5) Administratrix

Otis, Isaac N
pg 36 (1880 Nov 5) deceased

Oviatt, A C
pg 89 (1887 Jan 15) Appraiser

Owen, Frank
pg 34 (1880 Apr 1) Appraiser

Owen, Thomas R Jr
pg 3 (1875 Nov 5) Judge; pg 4 (1875 Dec 20) Judge; pg 5 (1875 Nov 12) Judge; pg 6 (1876 May 8) Judge; pg 7 (1876 June 6) Judge; pg 8 (1876 June 20) Judge; pg 9 (1875 Dec 3) Judge; pg 10 (1876 Mar 13) Judge; pg 11 (1876 May 31) Judge; pg 12 (1877 Feb 20) Judge; pg 13 (1877 Feb 20) Judge; pg 14 (1877 Aug 23) Judge; pg 15 (1877 Oct 2) Judge

Parvell Cattle Co.
pg 92 (1887 Mar 23)

Paynter, Emory C
pg 90 (1887 Feb 14) deceased - no widow

Peck Lateral Ditch Co.
pg 89 (1887 Jan 15)

Pennock, A J
pg 70 (1885 Dec 15) Appraiser

Pennock, Porter R
pg 57 (1884 Sept 12) Appraiser

Periam, Jno
pg 39 (1881 Dec 31) account

Peterson, Augusta
pg 65 (1885 May 26) Administratrix

Peterson, Martin
pg 65 (1885 May 26) deceased - store at Magnolia

Pickel, John H
pg 53 (1884 May 19) Appraiser

Pine, B F
pg 55 (1884 Aug 20) Appraiser; pg 65 (1885 May 26) Appraiser

Pint, Elizabeth
pg 29 (1879 Sept 3) Administratrix

Pint, Philip
pg 29 (1879 Sept 3) deceased

Poor, M (Mrs)
pg 103 (1887 Nov 13) Administratrix

Potter, Howard H
pg 38 (1881 June 23) deceased - no widow

Potter, R B
pg 14 (1877 Aug 23) Appraiser

Preston, H W
pg 86 (1886 Nov 29) Appraiser

Prince, Hiram
pg 49 (1884 Feb 5) Appraiser

Raike, Walter
pg 69 (1885 Dec 31) Appraiser

Ramsay, John
pg 89 (1887 Jan 15) Appraiser; pg 95 (1887 Apr 18) Appraiser

Rand, George
pg 81 (1886 June 28) Appraiser

Ransom, Daniel
pg 19 (1878 Apr 15) Appraiser

Rearden, Geo W
pg 59 (1884 Nov 8) Notary Public; pg 90 (1887 Feb 14) Notary Public

Reed, A
pg 31 (1880 Jan 21) note

Reed, Andrew
pg 10 (1876 Mar 13) Appraiser; pg 31 (1880 Jan 21) Appraiser

Reed, John
pg 77 (1886 May 20) Appraiser

Reese, John
pg 68 (1885 Sept 8) Administrator; pg 83 (1886 Sept 13) Appraiser; pg 98 (1887 May 23) deceased

Reese, Kate A
pg 98 (1887 May 23) Administratrix

Renslow, Samuel M
pg 2 (1875 Apr 14) deceased

Rhoades, J B
pg 95 (1887 Apr 18) account

Rich, Frank
pg 95 (1887 Apr 18) account

Richardson, Frederick
pg 8 (1876 June 20) deceased

Richart, Thos
pg 80 (1886 July 28) Appraiser

Rippey, W C
pg 64 (1885 May 4) note

RMN Bank
pg 4 (1875 Dec 20) note owed

Robinson, D A
pg 96 (1887 Apr 25) Appraiser

Rogers, Elizabeth R
pg 103 (1887 Nov 13) deceased

Rogers, George
pg 87 (1887 Jan 20) Judge; pg 88 (1887 Jan 25) Judge; pg 89 (1887 Jan 15) Judge; pg 90 (1887 Feb 14) Judge; pg 91 (1887 Mar 15) Judge; pg 92 (1887 Mar 23) Judge; pg 93 (1887 Apr 14) Judge; pg 95 (1887 Apr 18) Judge; pg 96 (1887 Apr 25) Judge; pg 97 (1887 May 4) Judge; pg 98 (1887 May 23) Judge; pg 99 (1887 July 22) Judge; pg 100 (1887 Sept 7) Judge; pg 101 (1887 Sept 12) Judge; pg 102 (1887 Sept 16) Judge; pg 103 (1887 Nov 13) Judge; pg 104 (1887 Nov 12) Judge; pg 105 (1887 May 23) Judge

Boulder County Appraisement Book A, 1875–1888

Rogers, Platt
pg 39 (1881 Dec 31) Appraiser

Rosenbaum, Chris
pg 56 (1884 Sept 15) Appraiser

Rosenbaum, M
pg 87 (1887 Jan 20) Appraiser

Rosenbaum, Michael
pg 56 (1884 Sept 15) Appraiser

Rosenkrans, Henry B
pg 14 (1877 Aug 23) Appraiser

Roth, Charlotte M
pg 105 (1887 May 23) Administratrix

Roth, James E
pg 105 (1887 May 23) deceased

Rough & Ready Ditch Co.
pg 39 (1881 Dec 31)

Rouse, Chas C
pg 91 (1887 Mar 15) Administrator

Rouse, Ella A
pg 91 (1887 Mar 15) deceased

Rowland, E
pg 29 (1879 Sept 3) Appraiser

Rowland, H E
pg 64 (1885 May 4) Notary Public

Rush, James
pg 95 (1887 Apr 18) account

Russell, Horace W
pg 37 (1881 June 6) Appraiser

Rutter, James G
pg 16 (1878 Feb 18) Appraiser

Sacket, Andrew
pg 99 (1887 July 22) Appraiser

Salsbury, M D
pg 20 (1878 May 31) Appraiser

Sawdy, Ared E
pg 49 (1884 Feb 5) deceased

Sawdy, Edgar
pg 49 (1884 Feb 5) Administrator; pg 88 (1887 Jan 25) Appraiser

Schellening, John L
pg 19 (1878 Apr 15) Justice of the Peace

Schmitt, John
pg 83 (1886 Sept 13) deceased

Schriver, J C
pg 91 (1887 Mar 15) Appraiser

Scott, William
pg 4 (1875 Dec 20) Appraiser

Seal, George
pg 65 (1885 May 26) Appraiser

Searcy, H
pg 95 (1887 Apr 18) account

Sears, George
pg 3 (1875 Nov 5) Administrator

Sears, Werley & Co
pg 3 (1875 Nov 5) Caribou business

Sears, William F
pg 3 (1875 Nov 5) deceased

Secor, Frank P
pg 48 (1884 Jan 28) Notary Public;
pg 57 (1884 Sept 12) Notary Public;
pg 74 (1886 Apr 23) Notary Public;
pg 88 (1887 Jan 25) Notary Public;
pg 89 (1887 Jan 15) Notary Public;
pg 97 (1887 May 4) Notary Public

Secor, N M
pg 102 (1887 Sept 16) Appraiser

Secor, William W
pg 7 (1876 June 6) Appraiser

Selkirk, Catherine
pg 20 (1878 May 31) Executrix

Selkirk, Edward A
pg 20 (1878 May 31) deceased

Severns, M
pg 39 (1881 Dec 31) account

Shade, Adam
pg 7 (1876 June 6) Appraiser

Shanahan, Michael
pg 50 (1884 Feb 11) Appraiser; pg 51 (1884 May 10) Appraiser

Shanahan, Timothy
pg 51 (1884 May 10) Administrator

Shaw, Joseph
pg 3 (1875 Nov 5) Appraiser

Sherwood, Clarence A
pg 2 (1875 Apr 14) Appraiser

Shull, J C
pg 39 (1881 Dec 31) account

Shull, Martin L
pg 42 (1882 Aug 23) Justice of the Peace

Shute, F A
pg 78 (1886 July 6) Conservator; pg 79 (1886 July 6) Conservator

Sibley, I D
pg 63 (1885 May 9) Appraiser

Sigley, William B
pg 57 (1884 Sept 12) Appraiser

Simmons, Johanna
pg 93 (1887 Apr 14)

Simpson, John H
pg 40 (1882 Feb 27) Appraiser

Simpson, William
pg 40 (1882 Feb 27) Appraiser

Sioux City Nursery
pg 95 (1887 Apr 18) account

Sites, William
pg 68 (1885 Sept 8) Appraiser; pg 98 (1887 May 23) Appraiser

Smith, A M
pg 39 (1881 Dec 31) account

Smith, C W
pg 78 (1886 July 6) Justice of the Peace; pg 79 (1886 July 6) Justice of the Peace

Smith, Estelle T Hinman
pg 80 (1886 July 28) Administratrix (see also Hinman, Estelle T)

Boulder County Appraisement Book A, 1875–1888

Smith, K
pg 95 (1887 Apr 18) account

Smith, N K
pg 92 (1887 Mar 23) Appraiser

Smith, R N
pg 75 (1886 Apr 5) Appraiser; pg 92 (1887 Mar 23) Appraiser

Smith, Thos S
pg 21 (1878 July 15) Justice of the Peace

Snyder, Hanson
pg 15 (1877 Oct 2) Appraiser

South Bluff Ditch Co.
pg 68 (1885 Sept 8)

Spencer, C L
pg 96 (1887 Apr 25) Appraiser

Spillers, B F
pg 4 (1875 Dec 20) note owed - second on Idaho Lode property

Spruce, J B
pg 26 (1878 Dec 14) Appraiser

St Clair, Dave
pg 95 (1887 Apr 18) account

St Clair, Joel T
pg 63 (1885 May 9) Appraiser

Staats, John Cuyler
pg 15 (1877 Oct 2) Administrator

Standley, D N
pg 95 (1887 Apr 18) account

Stanfield, A F
pg 61 (1884 Dec 18) deceased

Stapp, I S
pg 90 (1887 Feb 14) Appraiser

State Bank of Boulder
pg 39 (1881 Dec 31)

Steamboat Springs Co.
pg 64 (1885 May 4)

Steers, Charles B
pg 60 (1884 Nov 24) Appraiser; pg 61 (1884 Dec 18) Appraiser

Stewart, J C
pg 28 (1879 Aug 15) Appraiser; pg 36 (1880 Nov 5) Appraiser

Stewart, John F
pg 99 (1887 July 22) Administrator

Stewart, John F Jr
pg 99 (1887 July 22) Appraiser

Stickney, Frank H
pg 102 (1887 Sept 16) Notary Public; pg 102 (1887 Sept 16) Administrator

Stidger, George
pg 62 (1885 Apr 1) Appraiser

Stiles, Elwood W
pg 77 (1886 May 20) deceased

Stiles, Lillian B
pg 77 (1886 May 20) Administratrix

Stinchfield, George B
pg 15 (1877 Oct 2) deceased - of Orodelfan, Colo

Strickland, Geo
pg 95 (1887 Apr 18) account

Boulder County Appraisement Book A, 1875–1888

Strock, David B
pg 67 (1885 Aug 21) Justice of the Peace; pg 85 (1886 Oct 19) Justice of the Peace

Sutherland, S B
pg 30 (1879 Dec 31) Appraiser

Switzer, J S
pg 66 (1885 July 29) Appraiser; pg 71 (1886 Mar 16) Appraiser

Tagumouth Lode
pg 79 (1886 July 6)

Temple, Edwin J
pg 64 (1885 May 4) note; pg 75 (1886 Apr 5) Executor; pg 91 (1887 Mar 15) Appraiser; pg 92 (1887 Mar 23) Executor

Terrell, Andrew
pg 43 (1883 Jan 2) deceased

Terry, Seth
pg 54 (1883 Dec 17) Appraiser; pg 72 (1886 Mar 3) Appraiser

Thompson, Guy V
pg 58 (1884 Oct 14) Appraiser

Thompson, J H
pg 45 (1883 Apr 30) Appraiser; pg 101 (1887 Sept 12) Justice of the Peace

Thompson, John B
pg 95 (1887 Apr 18) Appraiser

Thompson, Thomas J
pg 101 (1887 Sept 12) Administrator

Thompson, William H
pg 64 (1885 May 4) Executor

Thorne, T J
pg 98 (1887 May 23) Notary Public

Thorp, M
pg 95 (1887 Apr 18) account

Three Brothers Lode
pg 79 (1886 July 6)

Tierney, John
pg 4 (1875 Dec 20) note owed - claims that these notes are paid and settled

Tillotson, Levi
pg 26 (1878 Dec 14) Appraiser

Tomlinson, Jas B Jr
pg 90 (1887 Feb 14) Appraiser

Topliff, Joseph J
pg 97 (1887 May 4) Executor

Tourtellot, James B
pg 6 (1876 May 8) Appraiser

Town of Longmont
pg 39 (1881 Dec 31) account

Towner, Reuben E
pg 1 (1875 Apr 12) deceased

Tracy, D L
pg 48 (1884 Jan 28) Appraiser

True, Charles C
pg 8 (1876 June 20) Appraiser

Boulder County Appraisement Book A, 1875–1888

Turner, R
pg 4 (1875 Dec 20) note owed - secured by trust and on property of Mt City

Tyler, Clinton M
pg 64 (1885 May 4) note; pg 75 (1886 Apr 5) deceased; pg 92 (1887 Mar 23) deceased

Ulury, Lenard S
pg 93 (1887 Apr 14) Notary Public

Van Deren, A J
pg 71 (1886 Mar 16) Appraiser

Varney, N E
pg 60 (1884 Nov 24) Appraiser; pg 95 (1887 Apr 18) account

Vaughn, George O
pg 26 (1878 Dec 14) Deceased

Vaughn, H Lee (Mrs)
pg 26 (1878 Dec 14) Administratrix

Vaughn, J P
pg 101 (1887 Sept 12) Appraiser

Viele, Thomas J
pg 104 (1887 Nov 13) deceased - no widow

Wachter, H O
pg 77 (1886 May 20) Justice of the Peace; pg 83 (1886 Sept 13) Justice of the Peace; pg 98 (1887 May 23) Appraiser

Walden, Jos
pg 95 (1887 Apr 18) account

Walker, Edward S
pg 55 (1884 Aug 20) Clerk of the County Court; pg 56 (1884 Sept 15) Clerk of the County Court; pg 61 (1884 Dec 18) Clerk of the County Court; pg 62 (1885 Apr 1) Clerk of the County Court; pg 63 (1885 May 9) Clerk of the County Court; pg 64 (1885 May 4) Clerk of the County Court; pg 65 (1885 May 26) Clerk of the County Court; pg 66 (1885 July 29) Clerk of the County Court; pg 67 (1885 Aug 21) Clerk of the County Court; pg 68 (1885 Sept 8) Clerk of the County Court; pg 69 (1885 Dec 31) Clerk of the County Court; pg 70 (1885 Dec 15) Clerk of the County Court; pg 71 (1886 Mar 16) Clerk of the County Court; pg 72 (1886 Mar 3) Clerk of the County Court; pg 73 (1886 Mar 26) Clerk of the County Court; pg 74 (1886 Apr 23) Clerk of the County Court; pg 75 (1886 Apr 5) Clerk of the County Court; pg 76 (1886 June 2) Clerk of the County Court; pg 78 (1886 July 6) Clerk of the County Court; pg 79 (1886 July 6) Clerk of the County Court; pg 80 (1886 July 28) Clerk of the County Court; pg 81 (1886 June 28) Clerk of the County Court; pg 83 (1886 Sept 13) Clerk of the County Court; pg 84 (1886 Oct 2) Clerk of the County Court; pg 85 (1886 Oct 19) Clerk of the County Court; pg 86 (1886 Nov 29) Clerk of the County Court; pg 87 (1887 Jan 20) Clerk of the County Court; pg 88 (1887 Jan 25) Clerk of the County Court; pg 89 (1887 Jan

15) Clerk of the County Court; pg 90 (1887 Feb 14) Clerk of the County Court; pg 91 (1887 Mar 15) Clerk of the County Court; pg 93 (1887 Apr 14) Clerk of the County Court; pg 95 (1887 Apr 18) Clerk of the County Court; pg 96 (1887 Apr 25) Clerk of the County Court; pg 97 (1887 May 4) Clerk of the County Court; pg 98 (1887 May 23) Clerk of the County Court; pg 99 (1887 July 22) Clerk of the County Court; pg 100 (1887 Sept 7) Clerk of the County Court; pg 101 (1887 Sept 12) Clerk of the County Court; pg 102 (1887 Sept 16) Clerk of the County Court; pg 103 (1887 Nov 13) Clerk of the County Court; pg 104 (1887 Nov 12) Clerk of the County Court; pg 105 (1887 May 23) Clerk of the County Court

Wallace, George
pg 20 (1878 May 31) Appraiser

Wallace, J J
pg 49 (1884 Feb 5) Appraiser

Wallace, M W
pg 46 (1883 Dec 17) deceased

Wallace, Martha M
pg 46 (1883 Dec 17) Administratrix

Walters, Enoch
pg 81 (1886 June 28) deceased; pg 82 (1886 Sept 9) deceased

Ward, L A
pg 3 (1875 Nov 5) Justice of the Peace

Warren, Caroline
pg 64 (1885 May 4) note

Warren, J M
pg 64 (1885 May 4) note

Washburn, H E
pg 43 (1883 Jan 2) Appraiser

Webster, George W
pg 8 (1876 June 20) Appraiser; pg 68 (1885 Sept 8) Appraiser

Weese, John
pg 8 (1876 June 20) Appraiser

Welch, L J
pg 47 (1883 Oct 25) Appraiser

Wellman, Sylvanus
pg 1 (1875 Apr 12) Appraiser;m pg 6 (1876 May 8) Appraiser

Wells, John H
pg 7 (1876 June 6) Notary Public; pg 35 (1880 Apr 1) Justice of the Peace; pg 60 (1884 Nov 24) Notary Public; pg 60 (1884 Nov 24) Administrator; pg 61 (1884 Dec 18) Administrator; pg 61 (1884 Dec 18) Notary Public; pg 69 (1885 Dec 31) Judge; pg 70 (1885 Dec 15) Judge; pg 71 (1886 Mar 16) Judge; pg 72 (1886 Mar 3) Judge; pg 73 (1886 Mar 26) Judge; pg 74 (1886 Apr 23) Judge; pg 75 (1886 Apr 5) Judge; pg 76 (1886 June 2) Judge; pg 77 (1886 May 20) Judge; pg 78 (1886 July 6) Judge; pg 79 (1886 July 6) Judge; pg 80 (1886 July 28) Judge; pg 81 (1886 June 28) Judge; pg 82 (1886 Sept 9) Judge; pg 83 (1886 Sept 13) Judge; pg 84 (1886

Boulder County Appraisement Book A, 1875–1888

Oct 2) Judge; pg 85 (1886 Oct 19) Judge; pg 86 (1886 Nov 29) Judge

Werley, R J
pg 105 (1887 May 23) Appraiser

Whitcomb, O P
pg 64 (1885 May 4) Appraiser

Whitcomb, Truman
pg 16 (1878 Feb 18) Appraiser; pg 45 (1883 Apr 30) deceased

White, Eben
pg 86 (1886 Nov 29) Appraiser

White, Perry
pg 66 (1885 July 29) deceased

White, Rachel B
pg 66 (1885 July 29) Administratrix

White, William H
pg 18 (1878 Apr 11) Appraiser

Whiteley, Richard H Jr
pg 75 (1886 Apr 5) Notary Public; pg 100 (1887 Sept 7) Notary Public

Widner, Amos
pg 11 (1876 May 31) Appraiser

Wilcox, Charles P
pg 68 (1885 Sept 8) Justice of the Peace; pg 68 (1885 Sept 8) Appraiser; pg 98 (1887 May 23) Appraiser

Williams, Emily
pg 33 (1880 Feb 21) Administratrix

Williams, Nathaniel P
pg 33 (1880 Feb 21) deceased

Williams, Thomas
pg 35 (1880 Apr 1) Appraiser; pg 75 (1886 Apr 5) Appraiser

Williamson, George R
pg 1 (1875 Apr 12) Executor

Williamson, George W
pg 22 (1878 June 17) Appraiser

Williamson, Samuel
pg 22 (1878 June 17) Appraiser

Wilson, G W
pg 41 (1882 May 15) Justice of the Peace

Wilson, Henry C
pg 36 (1880 Nov 5) Appraiser

Wilson, James B
pg 5 (1875 Nov 12) Appraiser

Wilson, John M
pg 56 (1884 Sept 15) Justice of the Peace; pg 81 (1886 June 28) Justice of the Peace; pg 82 (1886 Sept 9) Justice of the Peace

Wilson, Lane
pg 95 (1887 Apr 18) account

Wolcott, A P
pg 103 (1887 Nov 13) Appraiser

Wolf, William C
pg 6 (1876 May 8) deceased

Wolff, Jas
pg 84 (1886 Oct 2) Appraiser; pg 69 (1885 Dec 31) Appraiser

Wood, Gardner P
pg 1 (1875 Apr 12) Appraiser

Woods, William M
pg 4 (1875 Dec 20) Justice of the Peace

Woodward, Robert J
pg 66 (1885 July 29) Appraiser

Worn, William
pg 4 (1875 Dec 20) deceased

Wright, Alpheus
pg 12 (1877 Feb 20) Appraiser; pg 27 (1879 Jan 15) Appraiser; pg 32 (1880 Feb 3) Appraiser

Wright, Charles H
pg 80 (1886 July 28) Justice of the Peace

Wright, T J
pg 26 (1878 Dec 14) Appraiser

Wyman, George E
pg 35 (1880 Apr 1) Appraiser

Yates, Joseph Esq
pg 41 (1882 May 15) Sheriff

Zweck, Geo
pg 95 (1887 Apr 18) account

Boulder County Appraisement Book A, 1875–1888

Boulder County Appraisement Book A, 1875–1888

Boulder County Appraisement Book A, 1875–1888

www.ingramcontent.com/pod-product-compliance
Lightning Source LLC
Chambersburg PA
CBHW061519040426
42450CB00008B/1689